Dodos

by Melissa Higgins

Consulting Editor: Gail Saunders-Smith, PhD

Content Consultant: Margaret M. Yacobucci, PhD
Education and Outreach Coordinator,
Paleontological Society; Associate Professor,
Department of Geology, Bowling Green State University

CAPSTONE PRESS
a capstone imprint

Pebble Plus is published by Capstone Press,
1710 Roe Crest Drive, North Mankato, Minnesota 56003
www.capstonepub.com

Library of Congress Cataloging-in-Publication Data
Higgins, Melissa, 1953– author.
Dodos / by Melissa Higgins.
pages cm.—(Pebble Plus. Ice Age Animals)
Summary: "Describes the characteristics, food, habitat, behavior, and
extinction of dodos"—Provided by publisher.
Audience: Age 5–8.
Audience: Grades K to 3.
Includes bibliographical references and index.
ISBN 978-1-4914-2100-0 (library binding)
ISBN 978-1-4914-2318-9 (pbk.)
ISBN 978-1-4914-2341-7 (ebook pdf)
1. Dodo—Juvenile literature. 2. Extinct birds—Juvenile literature.
I. Title.
QL696.C67H54 2015
598.6'5—dc23   2014029101

Editorial Credits
Jeni Wittrock, editor; Peggie Carley and Janet Kusmierski, designers;
Wanda Winch, media researcher; Laura Manthe, production specialist

Photo Credits
Illustrator: Jon Hughes
Shutterstock: Alex Staroseltsev, snowball, April Cat, icicles, Konstanttin,
cover background, Leigh Prather, ice crystals, pcruciatti, interior background

Note to Parents and Teachers

The Ice Age Animals set supports national science standards related to life science. This
book describes and illustrates dodos. The images support early readers in understanding
the text. The repetition of words and phrases helps early readers learn new words.
This book also introduces early readers to subject-specific vocabulary words, which are
defined in the Glossary section. Early readers may need assistance to read some words
and to use the Table of Contents, Glossary, Read More, Internet Sites, and Index sections
of the book.

Printed in China by Nordica.
0914/CA21401504
092014   008470NORDS15

Table of Contents

Flightless 4

Made for Walking....................8

Life on the Ground 12

Dodo's End 16

Glossary.............................22

Read More...........................23

Internet Sites 23

Index 24

Flightless

A bird the size of a turkey walks through the forest. A sudden noise sends other birds into flight. But not the dodo. This bird can't fly.

Dodo birds lived only on Mauritius. This small island in the Indian Ocean had no predators. Safe on their island, dodos had no need to fly.

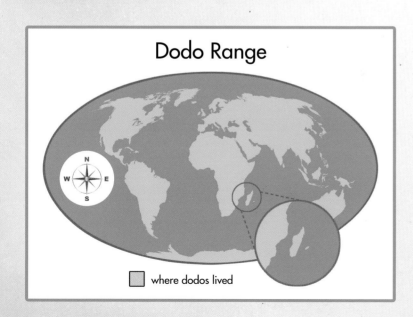

Dodo Range

☐ where dodos lived

Made for Walking

Over millions of years,

dodos' wings became small.

Dodos were too heavy to fly.

Instead they traveled on

their yellow legs.

Blue-gray feathers covered dodos' bodies. They had long, strong beaks. Dodos' closest living relatives are pigeons.

11

Life on the Ground

Dodos lived their entire lives on the forest floor. They ate fallen fruits and nuts. They may have also eaten fish.

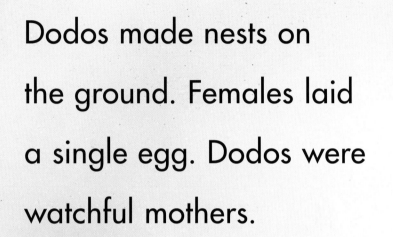

Dodos made nests on
the ground. Females laid
a single egg. Dodos were
watchful mothers.

Dodo's End

Dodos lived through the last Ice Age. Earth was cooler then, but ice and snow never reached Mauritius.

Sailors came to the dodo's island in 1598. Dodos walked right up to the men. The birds did not know to be afraid.

Sailors ate dodos for food.

The sailors' dogs and cats

hunted dodos and their eggs.

By 1693 the dodos had

become extinct.

Glossary

beak—the hard front part of the mouth of birds and some dinosaurs; also called a bill

extinct—no longer living; an extinct animal is one that has died out, with no more of its kind

Ice Age—a time when much of Earth was covered in ice; the last ice age ended about 11,500 years ago

predator—an animal that hunts other animals for food

relative—part of the same family

sailor—a person who works on a boat

Read More

Brecke, Nicole and Patricia M. Stockland. *Extinct and Endangered Animals You Can Draw.* Ready, Set, Draw! Minneapolis: Millbrook Press, 2010.

Ehrlich, Fred. *You Can't See a Dodo at the Zoo.* Maplewood, N.J.: Blue Apple Books, 2011.

Higgins, Melissa. *Woolly Mammoths.* Ice Age Animals. North Mankato, Minn.: Capstone Press, 2015.

Internet Sites

FactHound offers a safe, fun way to find Internet sites related to this book. All of the sites on FactHound have been researched by our staff.

Here's all you do:

Visit *www.facthound.com*

Type in this code: 9781491421000

 Super-cool stuff!

Check out projects, games and lots more at
www.capstonekids.com

Index

beaks, 10
bodies, 10
cats, 20
color, 8, 10
dogs, 20
eggs, 14, 20
extinct, 20
feathers, 10
flight, 4, 6, 8
food, 12
Ice Age, 16

legs, 8
Mauritius, 6, 16, 18
mothers, 14
nests, 14
pigeons, 10
predators, 6
relatives, 10
sailors, 18, 20
size, 4, 8
wings, 8

Word Count: 189
Grade: 1
Early-Intervention Level: 16